HELPING CHURCHES
TRANSFORM
COMMUNITIES

Matt Bird Publishing

PO Box 38082

London

SW19 1YW

UK

www.mattbirdpublishing.com

ISBN: 9798731580526

As a companion to this book we have created the

Cinnamon Transformation Course

available free at *cinnamonnetwork.com/courses*

Go deeper on the journey of transformation with other leaders from churches around the world.

Contents

Introduction

One of the frequent questions local churches ask about community transformation is, "Where should we start?" Or they ask, "What should we do next to serve the most vulnerable people?" Cinnamon Networks help local churches to discern where to start or what to do next by providing eight practical areas of support which the chapters of this book explore...

1. Knowing Your Why
The first is help knowing your 'why'. Clarity about the Biblical basis and motivation for church-led community transformation is critically important so that your expectations are God's expectations.

2. Discerning What To Do
Secondly, local churches want to know what to do in the community. So Cinnamon Network International has created a Community Transformation Pathway which is a five-question journey to help you discern what Jesus wants you to do in your neighbourhood or city.

3. Learning From Others
The third help is access to a menu of brilliant church-led community projects that you can take 'off the shelf' and adapt in your own community. These Cinnamon Recognised Projects are tried and tested models so they increase your effectiveness and avoid you having to 'reinvent the wheel'.

4. Strengthening Your Partnerships

Fourthly, local churches are increasingly developing unity for the purpose of community transformation. Our Church Unity Ladder helps local churches understand the relationship they have with one another, the impact that has on the community and how they can step up to the next rung of unity for transformation.

5. Praying for Transformation

The fifth help is an approach to praying for the wellbeing and transformation of the community. The Civic Prayer Breakfast model offers a five-step process for bringing together church leaders and civic leaders of all faiths and none to pray to Jesus for the well-being of your community.

6. Measuring Your Impact

We explore the importance of measuring social impact as part of the sixth step. The Cinnamon Faith Action Audit is a five-phase process for enabling local churches to work together to provide evidence that 'faith is a force for good'. This results in greater impact through increased influence, collaboration and resources.

7. Replicating What Works

If your local church runs a brilliant community project that other local churches might also be interested in running why not intentionally replicate it? The Cinnamon Community Project Replicator helps local-churches develop four benefits and build eight capabilities that enables you to replicate your model through other local churches.

8. Transformational Business

Local churches can provide economic solutions to economic crisis' within a community. The Cinnamon Spirit of Enterprise Hub provides a three dimensional support to people with ideas to create businesses that build human flourishing and thriving.

Our hope is that the support Cinnamon Network International offers will help your local church transform its community in new ways.

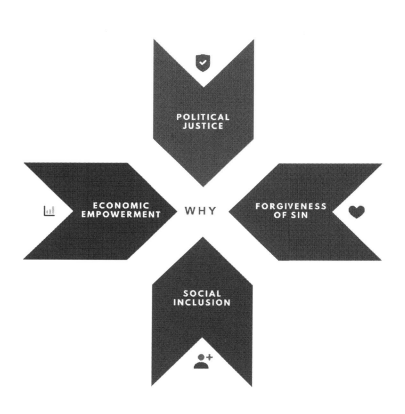

Session 1
Knowing Your Why

Why your church should be inspired to serve the community.

Knowing your 'why' is so important. At the start of Jesus's public work he said, "Repent, for the kingdom of heaven has come near." *(Matthew 3:2l)*. He then lived a life of sacrifice and transformation through which he:

- Offered the forgiveness of sin and a new start for absolutely anyone who would embrace him.
- Loved and socially included people who were culturally scorned and written off by the religious right.
- Economically empowered people by healing them of their diseases so they were whole and could work for a living and be saved the indignity of begging.
- Challenged political injustice by doing good on the Sabbath: forgiving the woman who was about to be killed and including lepers who society had segregated.

The Kingdom of God that Jesus declared and demonstrated really was good news. Interestingly, Jesus didn't say 'believe A, B and C and you will go to heaven when you die'. In fact Jesus said that heaven was coming to earth *(Matthew 6:10 & Luke 17:21)* and a new heaven and a new earth is 'coming down' *(Revelation 21:2)*. Sometimes we get the direction of heaven round the wrong way. Following Jesus is not a transaction that gets us into heaven when we die but a heavenly transformation that happens in us and through us in the here and now.

Pastor and theologian Leslie Newbiggin said, "The local church is the hermeneutic of the gospel." He meant that the local church demonstrates Jesus Christ to the wider community. The Message translation of the Bible said of Jesus, "He became flesh and blood and moved into the neighbourhood." *(John 1:14)*. What a beautiful picture of Jesus being alongside people.

Later on in the Book of John, Jesus said, "As the Father has sent me, I am sending you." *(John 20:21)*. So, in the same way that God sent Jesus into the world, Jesus now sends his church to be alongside people.

The Bible describes unconditional love when it says, "Whilst we were still sinners Christ died for us." *(Romans 5:8)*. There is nothing we can do to merit or deserve God's love and acceptance. How God has loved us is how we are encouraged to love other people. If we serve people just because we want them to come to Christ and come to church, they see the inauthenticity of our motives.

The Archbishop of Canterbury, Justin Welby, once described the work that Cinnamon Network helps churches do as 'provision wrapped in love'. Statutory social welfare struggles to deliver 'provision wrapped in love' because it is part of a bureaucratic machine in which professionals are specifically trained not to get emotionally involved with people. Some the most powerful provision is that delivered by people who have experienced the unconditional love of God themselves and are simply passing it forward.

At the same time as loving, caring and serving communities unconditionally, it is important to be ready to talk about the person who inspires us to do what we do. As the Apostle Peter says, "Always be prepared to give an answer to everyone who asks you to give the reason for the hope that you have." *(1 Peter 3:15).*

So, let's love people with no strings attached, regardless of whether they come to Christ or come to Church. Let's love people to bits because that is the extravagant nature of the love of God.

The experience of the Cinnamon Network International team in helping thousands of local churches on the journey of community transformation, is that the church has the greatest impact when it is motivated by Jesus's unconditional love

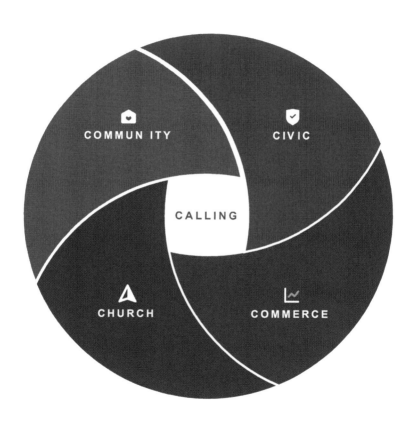

Session 2
Discerning What To Do

What Jesus is calling your church to do in the community.

In response to local churches increasingly wanting to know what to do in their community Cinnamon Network has developed a Community Transformation Pathway. The Community Transformation Pathway is a five-question journey to help you discern what Jesus is calling your local church to do to impact the community. The Pathway can be used by your church leadership team, community engagement working group, discipleship groups or the whole congregation.

Question 1: Community
What are the greatest social needs and resources in your community?

Genuine church-led community engagement starts with a profound understanding of the community. Begin by gaining an appreciation of the greatest felt needs and also the resources that exist amongst the community.

As more churches become engaged in their communities, there is a risk of local churches simply copying whatever seems to be popular and on trend. Jesus does not invite us to do what is fashionable but to genuinely serve.

There are a variety of ways that your church can find out what the deepest needs and resources of your community are. It is always beneficial to examine your local government's strategic plan because it will have already invested significantly in understanding the community's social needs and assets. Beyond that there are informal approaches of listening to people in the community: listen to what parents are saying at the school gates; what medical staff are saying in doctors surgeries and hospitals; and what people talk about at the pub or a local sports centre.

Bible Reflection:
Read Luke 17:11-19.
What are the deep social needs Jesus saw in the community of lepers?

Community Reflection:
What can you hear, see and sense about the activity of your community?
Are there places in your neighbourhood that you, or your family, don't or wouldn't go? Why is this?
What local parks and public spaces are there in the community? Who does it appear these spaces were created for and who do you observe using them?
Who doesn't have a voice and why might this be the case? Who has power and who does not?
What topics of conversation concerning the neighbourhood keep coming up?

Question 2: Civic
Where statutory provision is the most under resourced and strained?

It is critically important to understand what other civic agencies, organisations and voluntary groups are already doing in the community. Understanding what is already happening, what areas are most stretched and where the gaps are ensures that your church compliments rather than competes with other good work.

Where churches work together across a community, one of the most powerful actions is to build a relationship with the Chief Executive and their team in local government. Ask them how the church can serve. When the churches genuinely serve the felt needs of a community, the more it will be trusted and included by civic leaders and institutions.

I have found it of great importance for civic leaders and institutions to understand why the Church does what it does in the community as being 'faith based not faith biased'. The Church is motivated by a love for Jesus, but it does so for people of all faiths and none — it is completely indiscriminate about who it serves. As it loves and serves unconditionally so it will be trusted more and the opportunities that come its way will grow.

Bible Reflection:
Read Jeremiah 29:4-14.
What was meant when God's people were told to 'seek the peace and prosperity of the city'?

Community Reflection:
Who are the civic leaders and institutions in your community? Where are they the most and least effective in the community?
What does the local government strategic plan identify as the greatest needs in the community and what programmes do they have to address them?
What public buildings are there in the neighbourhood? How do they serve the community and how could they be of greater service?
Who are the decision makers in your community? Who has a voice and why is their voice heard?

Question 3: Commerce

What social responsibility priorities do local businesses have and where is there potential synergy?

Big business and small business alike have become more socially conscious of the environment and community they are operating in. Start by talking with the business people in your church and then reach out to other business leaders in the community about what areas of social responsibility their business has adopted.

Generally businesses will have determined some priority social issues which they focus on to express their responsibility and citizenship. Businesses may offer pro bono services, make gifts in kind, give community grants and encourage their workforce to donate time to community organisations. So local business can be a key partner for anyone who wants to serve their local community.

Bible Reflection:
Acts 16:13-15.
What are the resources that a business or business leader might have to share with others?

Community Reflection:
What are the two or three most significant business sectors that are present in your community?

Who are the entrepreneurial business owners who live and/or work locally? What is their heart to give back to the local community?

What big corporate businesses have local offices in your community and what are their corporate social responsibility priorities?

Where in your community do SME (Small and Medium sized Enterprises) meet together to support one another and how could you engage with them in that place?

Question 4: Church

What resources, assets and capabilities does your local church have that it can offer on a sustainable basis?

Trust and trusting relationships are built when we are consistent in our behaviour. So whatever your church starts in the community, it should be able to continue and sustain rather than run out of energy after a few months. If not it will actually do more harm than good.

Think through the resources that your church can commit on an ongoing sustainable basis:

- How much money can you budget for community service?
- How many volunteers are interested in serving?
- How many hours a week could volunteers give?
- What expertise and experience do your volunteers have?
- What building space could be used to serve the community?

It is also critically important that you understand what other local churches are doing in the community. In this way you ensure that what you do aligns or compliments rather than duplicates. Chapter 4 explores how local churches can work together for the benefit of their communities.

Bible Reflection:
Read Acts 6:1-7.
What resources, assets and capabilities did the early church have that it could share with others?

Community Reflection:
What are the most effective things that your church has done in the community in the last 12 months?
Who are the people in your church who have the most and the least discretionary time to serve in the community?
What skills and experience does your church have that are currently under-used for the community?
If your church has a building, how could it be utilised more to serve the community rather than internal activities?
What does your church's budget say about its missional priorities? What is the balance of church budget spent on Sunday meetings compared to the local community?

Question 5: Calling
What community need is Jesus calling your local church to do something about?

Understanding community needs, existing civic provision, commercial social responsibility, and church resources provides the information you need to more deeply consider how Jesus is calling your church to serve the community.

As followers of Jesus, you may want to pray in your Sunday worship, in small groups and with the leadership team about what Jesus is asking of you. There will also be times to discuss with others as well as go away and reflect before making a decision.

It may also be helpful to look at the menu of Cinnamon Recognised Projects, which I look at in Chapter 4 to consider some of the options available to you.

Once you discern the calling of Jesus it is time for action and commitment. As the Bible says, 'faith without action is dead', so ensure that you get beyond the important work of pondering and praying into activating and action. Our faith is one that has its sleeves rolled up and is ready to get involved.

Bible Reflection:
Read Acts 16:6-10.
How have you experienced Jesus leading and guiding you?

Community Reflection:
What sense of connection do you feel to the neighbourhood?

Where are the places of life, hope, beauty, joy and positive relationships in the neighbourhood?

What evidence of struggle, despair, neglect and alienation do you see? Who is suffering and why?

Where do you sense God has been, is currently and might want to be at work in your community?

Keeping On

Discerning what Jesus is calling your local church to do in the community is not an end state, but an ongoing journey. We would encourage you to continue listening, learning and leading:

- Listening: what are you hearing God and others say?
- Learning: how you are being challenged and changed by the journey?
- Leading: where are you finding a way through the complexity to a greater place of togetherness?

If you are enjoying this book so far, you can go deeper
on this transformation journey by signing up for our
Cinnamon Transformation Course,
available free at

cinnamonnetwork.com/courses

*Discerning what Jesus is calling
your local church to do
is an ongoing journey
of listening, learning and leading...*

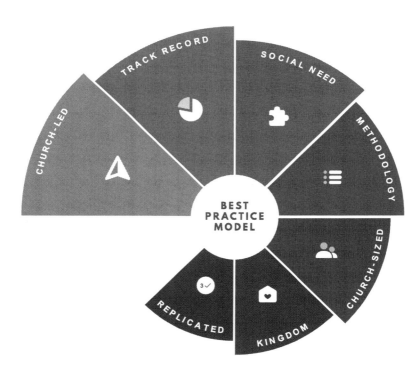

Session 3
Learning From Others

What other churches are doing effectively that you could benefit from.

Local churches are doing amazing work in communities around the world to demonstrate Jesus's love to people experiencing vulnerability.

Brilliant Models

Some of the brilliant examples of church-led community transformation that we have discovered and are working with are:

- Circuit Breaker (Australia): Helps local churches reduce domestic violence through a prevention programme focused on helping people who feel their anger is beginning to damage their relationships.
- Adopt-a-Police Team (South Africa): Helps local churches reduce crime by enabling them to adopt a local police station which they can serve, pray for and work alongside in the community.
- Steps (Denmark): Helps local churches reduce addiction by supporting them to run a change programme to free people from addictive behaviours.
- Peaced Together (United Kingdom): Helps local churches reduce vulnerability amongst women through

a programme which helps them talk through the pain in their lives and explore how they can be rebuilt.

The approach of Cinnamon Network in each country is to build a menu of outstanding church-led community projects that local churches can choose from to increase their effectiveness and impact. This also presents local churches from duplicating God-given resources by reinventing the wheel. You can check out the menu of brilliant community projects in your country by visiting cinnamonnetwork.com

If you think a project is what Jesus is calling your local church to do to impact your community, please reach out to them directly. They will be able to explain more about how they can help you transform community and what benefits they provide.

Best Practice

Cinnamon Network selects community projects for its menu against seven best practice criteria that have produced the best results.

We call these community projects Cinnamon Recognised Projects, as they come with our recommendation and endorsement to provide you peace of mind. The criteria are:

- Local church-led (rather than individual-led).
- Track-record for changing lives (rather than a good idea).
- Effectively address a specific social need (rather than being generally good).

- Core methodology that can be replicated (rather than a charismatic leader that cannot).
- Average local church sized (rather than requiring a big and resourceful church).
- Kingdom hearted and minded (rather than obsession with empire, ego and logo).
- Replicated in a minimum of three local churches (rather than being a solo project).

Potential Community Projects

You may know of a brilliant church-led community project that you think has the potential to be a Cinnamon Recognised Project, which we would love to hear about.

If the community project meets all seven best practice criteria, Cinnamon Network will consider inviting them to become a Cinnamon Recognised Project.

If they meet the first six criteria but not the — i.e. they have not yet replicated in three or more local churches — Cinnamon Network may invite them to join our Cinnamon Community Project Replicator to help them do just that.

If you think you might have a church-led community project that would be of interest to us, please contact Cinnamon Network via our website to examine the local government strategic plan, because they will have already invested significantly in understanding their communities. cinnamonnetwork.com/contact

Let's build a menu of brilliant church-led community projects that local churches can choose from to increase their impact and prevent them from reinventing the wheel

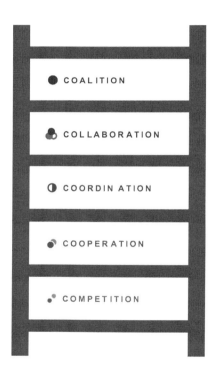

LADDERS

COALITION

COLLABORATION

COORDIN ATION

COOPERATION

COMPETITION

SNAKES

Session 4

Strengthening Your Partnerships

How churches can work together in community transformation.

As local churches become more focused on community transformation, they are also discovering one another and choosing to journey together to pursue the peace and prosperity of their village, town or city *(Jeremiah 29:7)*.

Cinnamon Network describes these emerging collectives of leaders and congregations as 'local church networks'. Each network is on a unique journey of growing unity for the purpose of greater community transformation. Our team has been involved in supporting the development of local church networks in communities and cities around the world. Our experience has led us to develop the Cinnamon Church Unity Ladder which explains the different sorts of relationships between churches in the community. These range from the highly undesirable to the desirable.

Rung 1: Competition

On the first rung of the Cinnamon Church Unity Ladder, local churches in a district or a city feels like they are jostling with one another to attract attendees and members. Local church logos and egos are, sadly, at the forefront as they compete with one another for members. The churches work in isolation from each other, often with prejudice about the other's beliefs and practices.

Cinnamon Network is working in a city where there is a history of competition between the churches. At one stage, key church leaders, who had not met each other, not only refused to talk to each other, but they would openly criticise each other's theology and practices. Thankfully, these leaders have since met and have started to build good relations.

Rung 2: Co-operation

The second rung of local church unity is when churches have decided they have a common purpose in the community for the benefit of residents. Church leaders are building relationships with one another, eating, drinking and praying together. Leaders choose to speak well of each other, both inside and outside the room.

Cinnamon Network has been involved in facilitating co-operation between local church leaders in many districts and cities in order to help them find their common purpose. In one of those settings, there was a moment of surprise when one of the leaders suggested they raised their commitment to co-operate by meeting together once a month. They now meet monthly for breakfast, relationships and prayer.

Rung 3: Co-ordination

On the third rung of local church unity, leaders realise none of them are big enough to address all the needs of the community, so agree to work together in a complimentary way. They co-ordinate which local church does what activity in the community and begin to cross refer community beneficiaries, and sometimes even volunteers, between different local churches.

Cinnamon Networks develop a menu of Cinnamon Recognised Projects that local churches can choose from and then locally adapt for their context (as was explained in chapter 3). In any community, district or city, no one church is big enough to run all the community projects to address all the most pressing social needs. So, it is normal that local churches co-ordinate who does what in the community.

Rung 4: Collaboration

The fourth rung represents the phase of unity where local churches recognise that whilst there are many things they can do in a co-ordinated fashion, there are some things that they can only do together.

Cinnamon Networks have helped the local churches in many communities and cities start a Civic Prayer Breakfast (as will be explained in chapter 5). Churches collaborate to host an event in their town hall or other civic venue in order to pray for the community. Civic leaders are invited to pray for seven sectors:

- Business and Finance
- Education and Learning
- Health and Well-being
- Media, arts and Entertainment
- Government and Politics
- Policing and Security
- Community and Family

There is more information about Civic Prayer Breakfasts in the next chapter.

Rung 5: Coalition

On the fifth rung of unity, churches create an alliance and consortium to work together to address specific social issues in the community. This often involves working more closely with civic leaders and institutions, having made the case that they are a force for good in the community. There will often be a single point of contact from the churches to civic leaders and institutions in order to making coalition working possible.

Cinnamon Network supports the churches in communities and cities to work together to measure their social impact through the Cinnamon Faith Action Audit (as will be explained in chapter 6). By learning to become bilingual and communicate the church's value in numbers, as well as the stories, the church is able to engage in new ways with civic leaders and institutions.

The Chief Executive of one city government was asked to comment on the results of the Cinnamon Faith Action Audit. They expressed their amazement about how much the church was doing (the church was also amazed). They explained that there were so many churches that it would be impossible for the city government to work with each of them and asked if the churches might work together as one church? The church leaders were stunned and humbled by the suggestion, but agreed to form a coalition to be the conduit between the churches and the city. The church coalition and the city government have now identified six areas of common concern that they are working on together.

Snakes and Ladders

Local church networks are not static but dynamic. The attitudes and behaviours of church leaders towards one another can be like snakes, creating greater distrust and disunity, or like ladders, building the opportunity for greater trust and unity. What attitudes and behaviours have you seen that increase unity and decrease unity?

There are times and seasons of unity, sometimes there are social and environmental factors that bring the church together. A sudden increase in the number of refugees arriving in the city can trigger the local church network to form a coalition to ensure that each refugee is welcomed and supported on the journey of integrating. A disaster in the community may bring church leaders together to respond with immediate frontline support to those effected and also the emergency services.

Your Unique Network

Every local church network is unique so you are not going to fit into anyone else's box. This Cinnamon Church Unity Ladder is designed to help leaders reflect more deeply about where your local church network is on your journey and where you could develop next. You may find the following transitions helpful in developing to the next stage:

Transition 1: Competition to Co-operation

Invite local church leaders to meet together initially, then regularly, around a commitment to the person of Jesus Christ and his mission of community transformation. Whilst we all hold other important theological distinctions for the sake of unity, we can accept they are secondary. For example, you might agree to form a local church network.

Transition 2: Co-operation to Co-ordination

Invite local church leaders to develop a sense of unity for purpose to start working together for the transformation of community. Initially, this can get underway by a commitment to co-ordinate who does what in the community and to ensure that efforts are complimentary rather than duplicated. For example, you might co-ordinate who runs which Cinnamon Recognised Project in the community to ensure there is a breadth of provision.

Transition 3: Co-ordination to Collaboration

Invite local church leaders to consider one thing they could decide to do together for the benefit of the community. Collaborating on a community-wide or city-wide project that has a defined start and end point will be a sense of shared achievement, relational trust and confidence in collective action. For example, you might form a collaboration to host a Civic Prayer Breakfast to praying for the well-being of the community or city, which could become an annual event.

Transition 4: Collaboration to Coalition

Invite local church leaders to consider creating a community-wide or city-wide alliance to research your current situation, and then tackle a specific social issue. For example, you might form a coalition to undertake a Faith Action Audit and then work with the local government to address a social need, such as finding foster and adoption families for children who are currently in temporary care.

Oneness

Jesus was clear that that oneness is pivotal to the success of what he has asked us to be and do in communities. He prayed that the Church might be one that the world might believe *(John 17:20-23)*. Cinnamon Network prays that your local church network might be one, so that the Church in your community becomes more believable and transformational.

There are times and seasons of unity. Sometimes there are social and environmental factors that can bring the church together

Session 5
Praying For Transformation

How churches can pray together for the transformation of your community.

As followers of Jesus, we don't believe in the power of prayer — we believe in the power of God! Prayer puts us in a place where God can do a work of transformation in us and our communities. What is one of the most effective ways to pray for community transformation?

The story of Jonah is a wonderful example of city transformation. After some resistance, Jonah finally followed God's request to go to the city of Nineveh and communicate his heart to them in a way they would understand. As a result, the King called the city to prayer and said, "Who knows? God may yet relent and with compassion turn from his fierce anger so that we will not perish." *(Jonah 3:9)*. So how can we communicate God's heart to our cities and invite them to pray?

Civic Prayer Breakfasts are a powerful way of expressing God's heart to the leaders of our communities and cities. Cinnamon Network has developed a Civic Prayer Breakfast model as a highly effective way to bring church leaders together with civic leaders to pray for the well-being of the community or city.

Civic Prayer Breakfasts have been run by hundreds of leaders in communities and cities around the world, and change and transformation has followed. Church leaders and civic leaders alike describe their Civic Prayer Breakfast as one of the most strategic events in their annual calendar. Here are the five-steps for hosting a Civic Prayer Breakfast...

Step 1: Vision Ownership

From the beginning, gain the widest possible involvement and ownership for the vision of your Civic Prayer Breakfast. Identify the most influential church leaders in your community and meet them on a one to one basis to gain their commitment. If you have a regular meeting of a local church network, present the vision and ask them to commit — it is helpful to gain the commitment of the key influencers first. It will help develop ownership if you then form a 'Civic Prayer Breakfast Team' of the most enthusiastic people.

Step 2: Civic Relationships

One of the key benefits of a Civic Prayer Breakfast is an opportunity to initiate and/or strengthen relationships with civic leaders across your community. The Civic Prayer Breakfast is also a means to an end, not an end in itself. This is your opportunity to build relationships for the event and long-term future.

Write a list of the most influential leaders you know or know of. You may find it helpful to use the Cinnamon Seven Sector framework:

- Business and Finance
- Education and Learning
- Health and Well-being
- Media, Arts and Entertainment
- Politics and Government
- Police and Security
- Community and Family

Start with the civic leaders you have established the most trust with first before going to others; meet and ask them if they will be a part of the initiative. You can then move on to those you don't know so well, but by then, you will have some natural momentum from others that you have spoken with.

When you meet for a coffee, listen more than you talk. Seek to understand their world and where they are under the most pressure in their work. Explain that you are hosting a civic event in which you are going to pray for the needs of the community and ask if they would be interested in attending. Send them a formal invitation. Depending on who they are, you might like to ask them to become involved in the programme in some way.

Step 3: Planning Team

With your Civic Prayer Breakfast planning team, it will be beneficial to recruit passionate and skilled people who can deliver the very best event. We recommended that you consider having team members responsible for logistics, communications, and programmes. Here are some check-lists that you may find helpful.

Programme Suggested Check-List

• Breakfast & Relationships. One of the best ways to build relationships with others is to eat and drink together. While you will not have time for a long and lingering breakfast, don't rush people because it's as they eat and drink that relationships will be built.

• Prayer. Make the prayers interesting and accessible. Focus on praying for the community and the points raised by civic leaders when you ask them about their greatest needs. Ask civic leaders to pray, if they are not used to praying in public they could use a written prayer or simple liturgy. You can also invite a designated person to pray at each table.

• Interviews. This is a powerful opportunity for two or three people to tell the story of how God is at work in their workplace or to be asked, "What keeps you awake at night?" This could be a teacher, police officer, business entrepreneur or any leader who has a heart for community transformation.

• **Say 'thank you'.** Use the Civic Prayer Breakfast as an opportunity to publicly honour and appreciate leaders who work tirelessly for others who are rarely thanked and appreciated. You might like to give a token gift or even make a public service award.

• **Civic Speaker.** The right civic speaker can help bring credibility and appeal to your event. You will probably prefer someone who is going to appeal to the widest possible constituency and inspire people without delivering a sermon.

• **Sung Worship.** If you plan to include some sung worship in your programme, keep it simple and use well-known hymns/songs that those people who don't regularly go to church might know.

Sample programme:

07:00 Guests arrive
07:30 Welcome & Opening Prayer
07:35 Breakfast & Relationships
08:05 Sung Worship
08:10 Interviews
08:25 Prayer
08:30 Civic Speaker
08:50 Table host-led prayers or discussion
09:00 Say 'Thank You'
09:10 Closing Remarks including date for next years event & Prayer
09:15 Formal Close

Logistics Suggested Check-List

• Venue: Host the Civic Prayer Breakfast in a civic building or hotel (rather than a church) to help make the event inclusive.

• Parking/Transportation: Think ahead about how people will travel to the event and if they are driving where they can park.

• Guests: Be confident about inviting civic leaders of all faiths and none. The Civic Prayer Breakfast is designed as a cross-over event centred on Jesus.

• Welcome Team: Recruit a team of the warmest and friendliest people to welcome guests as they arrive and register them.

• Table Plan: A table plan can help avoid chaos when people sit down. The easiest way to organise this is when people register on arrival provide them with a badge with their table number on.

• MC: An experienced Master of Ceremonies will help the programme flow and keep to time.

• Catering: Eating and drinking together is a powerful way to get to know people, so provide a good breakfast.

• Table Hosts: Appoint a host at each table who can ensure everyone feels welcome and included throughout the event.

• Tickets: Charge for tickets because people value what they pay for. If you do not charge you will have a higher number of no-shows.

Communications Suggested Check-List

These ideas enable you to get the maximum value of your Civic Prayer Breakfast, although all may not be possible.

• Guest List: A single point of contact who is managing the RSVP list is essential so that no acceptances and apologies fall through the gap.

• Reminder: Sending a 'looking forward to seeing you' note prior to the event is a helpful way of ensuring you gain the best possible attendance.

• Thank You: Sending a 'thank you for attending' note after the event is a good opportunity to communicate what you plan to do next.

• News Release: A well crafted news release for local papers and local radio stations might result in journalists attending the event and/or reporting the story.

• Social Media: Livestream the Civic Prayer Breakfast and post about the event as it happens; this will help engage the millennial generation.

• Photographer: High quality photographs are one of the best ways to help tell the story of the Civic Prayer Breakfast and promote next years!

Step 4: The Event

Your Civic Prayer Breakfast is all about Jesus and the community. Create an environment that is non-partisan, where politicians are invited to leave their party politics at the door and pastors leave their important, but secondary, theological issues at their desks. The event is where you will pray and ask for God's help for the well-being and transformation of your community.

Step 5: Prayer Rhythm

You might like to use the Civic Prayer Breakfast to encourage people and churches to follow a fresh prayer rhythm, using the Cinnamon Seven Sector framework. Each day of the week can be focused prayer for leaders and organisations in a different sector of your community:

Monday: Business and Finance
Tuesday: Education and Learning
Wednesday: Health and Well-being
Thursday: Media, Arts and Entertainment
Friday: Politics and Government
Saturday: Police and Security
Sunday: Community and Family

This is a habit that you can adopt personally, with other leaders, your small group and church and/or across the whole community.

*Prayer places us where God
can do a work of transformation
both in us and
in our communities*

Session 6

Measuring Your Impact

How to measure the impact of local churches in the community.

The Church communicates value through the stories it tells. In contrast, civic society communicates value through the numbers and metrics it uses. Cinnamon Network helps the Church become bilingual by communicating its value in numbers as well as stories.

Developing the capability to communicate the value of what the Church and faith-based organisations do in numbers, transforms the way in which people perceive their contribution. What previously seemed soft, fluffy and nice becomes concrete, specific and real. Civic leaders and institutions – whether in government, police or business – who were agnostic about the role of church and faith in society will become advocates. This is what happens when the Church becomes bilingual.

Jesus told the parable of the talents in which a wealthy man gave one person five talents, another man received two talents and a third only one talent. The one who had been entrusted with five produced another five; the person who had been entrusted with two produced another two. The man who had been entrusted with one simply returned the one! *(Matthew 25:14).*

The investor was not only wealthy but wise, he had done his due diligence. His research confirmed that he was right to trust five talents to the man who had subsequently provided a 100% return. I can imagine he was surprised with the person who he had entrusted with three talents, who also provided 100% return on investment. Perhaps he should have also entrusted him with five? However, the one who given a single talent produced no return on investment, which was unacceptable.

Whether investing in a business, allocating resources for public service or donating to a non-profit, wise people want to know what their return on investment will be. In business, that return will be financial with increasing social expectations. In the public sector the return is social capacity alongside value for money. In non-profits, the return is the whole person and financial probity.

I believe this parable should cause us to ask what 'return on investment' are we showing the people who donate and partner with our local church or faith based organisation? Stories are powerful but so are metrics.

Byron Loflin, Vice-President at NASDAQ, responsible for Board engagement, says, "What's measured moves." It is my experience that what you measure becomes a compass and magnet for your time, energy, and resources. That is where growth and change happen. How do you measure the impact of your church or Christian organisation? What are your goals? Where is your time, energy, and resources expended? What change are you measuring?

Cinnamon Faith Action Audit

Cinnamon Network has developed the Cinnamon Faith Action Audit (CFAA), a unique tool for helping local churches in a community work together to measure their community impact.

It enables local churches to work together in a specific area to measure the contribution they make to the life of their communities. Whilst it measures many things, the lead metric is the monetary value of the time given by people from local churches and faith-based organisations to the community each year.

In the United Kingdom, the Cinnamon Faith Action Audit has been used by churches and faith groups in 92 government districts to measure their social and economic impact. The average respondent rate was 46.5%, and the data covers more than 20% of the UK population. The Times newspaper ran an article of the results from the UK-wide CFAA with the headline "Loving thy neighbour is priceless – but also worth £3billion" (per annum).

This research has made civic society sit up and listen to the Church and faith-based organisations like never before. It has elevated the confidence of the Church and civic society to collaborate in new ways. It has brought the Church and faith-based organisations to the table to be involved in the strategic planning of their communities. It has challenged the unity of the Church and to recognise the value of who they are as a united force for good. It has also resulted in government, business, police and health agencies making grants to church-led community development.

In 2019, the first US Cinnamon Faith Action Audits were completed in two New York City zip code areas: East New York and Washington Heights. This demonstrated that the human capital value of local churches and faith groups is worth $50million per annum. New York City has 176 zip codes, so when this data is extrapolated it values faith-based human capital at $8.8billion per annum. This is now transforming conversations the churches are having about their role in the life and future of the city.

Purpose and Benefits

Cinnamon Network supports local church networks in local government areas to complete a Cinnamon Faith Action Audit. The main purpose of the CFAA is to provide evidence that faith is a force for good and using that to gain greater influence, collaboration and resources. However, there are additional benefits including:

- Unifying the Church in the community with a greater sense of common purpose.
- Capturing the identity of who the churches in the community are together.
- Creating a benchmark against which future progress can be evaluated.

- Equipping God's people with a compelling story about the tangible impact of their faith.
- Providing public confidence that 'faith is a force for good'.
- Beginning or accelerating the community transformation journey.
- Identifying the most pressing needs and scale effective solutions.

The Process

The Cinnamon Faith Action Audit is a unique online-based tool for demonstrating that 'faith is a force for good' and involves a five-phase process from initial vision to final delivery.

Phase 1: Commitment

Gaining the commitment of the widest possible network of church leaders and other stakeholders for the purpose of a Faith Action Audit, and confirming the service agreement. If there are existing relationships with civic leaders, it is valuable to bring them into the picture at this stage as they will be excited about this initiative.

Phase 2: Database

Building, or building out, an extensive database of local churches and faith-based organisations within a defined local government area. The audience for the CFAA is civic society, so all places of worship and faith-based organisations are included in order that the case that faith is a force for good can be made.

Phase 3: Survey

The CFAA platform runs the survey for a calendar month with automated reminders. The key to obtaining a high respondent rate is mobilising a team of champions who work throughout the survey phase to explain why completing the survey is strategic.

Phase 4: Report

The CFAA platform analyses the data and produces a high quality report. Local images, leaders greeting and partner logos are added. The final report is signed off between Cinnamon Network and the local partner.

Phase 5: Launch

Launching the CFAA results through a civic event should also include PR, social media and word of mouth campaign.

Phase 6: Transformation Phase

The real work then begins as the CFAA evidence is used to accelerate how local churches work together in community transformation.

Church leaders and civic leaders become more engaged in strategic conversations and planning for the well-being and transformation of the community.

The Cinnamon Community Transformation Pathway (chapter 2) provides a powerful process for engaging communities, government agencies, businesses and churches to discern transformative action.

Cinnamon Network International helps the church become bilingual by communicating its value in both number metrics and stories

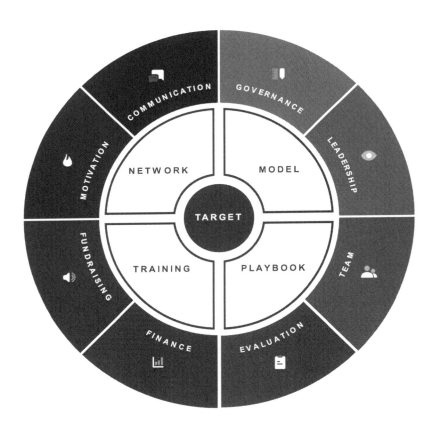

Session 7
Replicating What Works

How to replicate best practice through other local churches.

Our God-given time, energy, talents and resources are too valuable to waste reinventing the wheel. Why recreate a community project that another local church has already pioneered and refined? Why not adopt the best practice that has been developed by another local church and adapt it to fit in your context?

Cinnamon Network has pioneered a strategy of 'replication rather than duplication'.

We identify exceptional church-led community projects and help them to capture the genius of what they do and package it in a way that it can be given to other local churches.

The Cinnamon Community Project Replicator helps projects run by one local church replicate through a minimum of three other local churches.

The Replicator framework invites church-led community projects to set one target, develop four benefits and build eight capabilities.

The questions below are indicative of the areas that the Replicator journey helps community projects develop.

Set One Target

- Target: How many local churches would you like to replicate your community project in the next 12 months?

Develop Four Benefits

- Model: What social problem does your community project address and what is your tried and tested solution?
- Complete the proposition: < *name of your community project* > helps local churches to reduce < *name the social problem* > by supporting them to *<name the solution>*
- Training: What essential things do you need to pass on to others who want to plan, launch, deliver and sustain your community project?
- Playbook: What is the strategic plan, funding model, role descriptions, policies and procedures?
- Network: What do you commit to members of your network and what do your members commit to your network?

Build Eight Capabilities

- Governance: What community project oversight will build trust, create value, develop strategy, provide accountability, monitor performance and protect culture?
- Leadership: How do you keep in balance the need to develop self, financial and operational leadership?
- Team: What are your strengths and, therefore, what complimentary strengths do you need to recruit into your team?

- Evaluation: What is your primary outcome measurement and how do you ensure that data is collected?
- Finance: What are the financial management, controls, monitoring and reporting processes?
- Fundraising: How can you generate income (training, playbook, network and other) and how can you raise money (donations, sponsorship, grants and other)?
- Motivation: How do you help your team demonstrate Jesus's love without strings attached and at the same time be ready to talk about their hope?
- Communication: How do you use digital media to make your community project widely known amongst local churches?

Cinnamon Community Project Replicator

Cinnamon Replication Communities are hosted in countries around the world to support leaders of church-led community projects to replicate through other churches. The Replicator framework is used to analyse development needs and to coach and mentor partners. The initial target is to help church-led community projects be replicated in a minimum of three other local churches in the first year. Three replications validates a community project as replicable, after which it is only a matter of building capacity to replicate through 30, 300 or thousands of local churches.

If you know, or know of, a church-led community project that might fit what Cinnamon is doing we would love to hear from them cinnamonnetwork.com/contact

We identify brilliant church-led community projects and help them to capture the genius of what they do and package it in a way that it can be given to other local churches

PLAN
PEOPLE

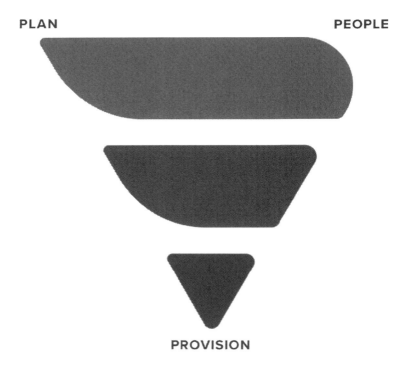

PROVISION

Session 8
Transformational Business

How to start businesses that transforms your community.

There is an old proverb which says, give someone a fish and you'll feed them for a day, teach them how to fish and you'll feed them for a lifetime.

Or to put it another way set up a local church food bank and you'll provide food parcels that feed a family for a few days, help a member of that family find work and you'll feed them for life.

Disasters such as the Covid-19 global pandemic create unemployment at unimaginable levels and drive families and communities into poverty.

Poverty can be relieved by charity, but the only sustainable solution to poverty is to create jobs and ethical business. In a crisis situation emergency relief deals with immediate needs but strategic development builds a new and enduring future.

The Bible says, "But remember the LORD your God, for it is he who gives you the ability to produce wealth, and so confirms his covenant, which he swore to your ancestors, as it is today." (Deuteronomy 8:18).

Clearly wealth creation is a gift of God and not a gift of capitalism.

The Cinnamon Spirit of Enterprise Hub enables local churches to support people with ideas, or people who want an idea, to start a business that creates human flourishing and thriving. The Enterprise Hub provides a plan, people and provision.

Plan

The plan provides a three stage process and funnel for reaching and supporting people who are interested in starting a business...

- Café: Host an Enterprise Café and bring together people from your church and community who have or would like an idea to start a business. During the café (which is very much an informal information session) take time to explain what enterprise is and how the Church believes it is a God-given gift. Explain the seven-session Enterprise Course and invite people if they would like to commit and take part.

- Course: Cinnamon Network provides course content including introductory short-films, session outlines, business templates and a leaders guide. The Enterprise Course walks people step-by-step through the process of conceiving, planning and launching a business.

- Co-working: At the end of the Enterprise Course, some participants will be ready to start a business, if they haven't already been inspired to do so. There are three ways that the church can enter into a Enterprise Co-working arrangement with them:

  1. Your church can create some open-plan business space where entrepreneurs can meet at least once a week, if not daily. Leaders and entrepreneurs often face loneliness and providing a place where they can mutually support one another is transformational.

  2. Secondly, your church could provide each person with an enterprise mentor. This is an opportunity for someone who is or has had a leadership role in business to give one hour a week to get behind an entrepreneur.

  3. Finally, your church could provide a small enterprise grant to help with the initial set-up costs of the business. The grant could be used for a computer, deposit on a vehicle, initial stock or other equipment.

People

There are three key people and roles in a Cinnamon Spirit of Enterprise Hub.

1. Participant: The participant is the person who has or wants to find an idea to start a business. It does not matter if there is already a business offering similar services; you only need to change a venture by 10% for it to become a new enterprise.

2. Facilitators: A lead volunteer is required to host the Enterprise Café, facilitate the Enterprise Course and lead the Enterprise Co-working. The volunteer does not need to be an expert, just confident in hosting, speaking and leading a group.

3. Mentors: The mentors must have experience of leading or managing a business. There are not many people who could not give one hour a week to meet with an emerging entrepreneur. The role of the mentor is to be sounding board and listening ear, as well as offering advice and experience.

Provision

Giving advice and insight as well as a place to work is essential and priceless, but setting up an enterprise comes at a price. There is an opportunity for churches to provide and catalyse the provision entrepreneurs need to launch, develop and grow their business.

• Start-up Grants: Churches can provide modest grants to emerging entrepreneurs to help them launch their business. The start-up grants can help entrepreneurs buy equipment, such as a computer or help buying stock.

• Stretch-out Contracts: Once the business has launched and is becoming established, there is an opportunity for it to stretch-out and grow. At this point there are often further employment opportunities. One of the ways this can be resourced is through profit share contracts, where an investor shares the risk and reward of the business with the entrepreneur.

• Scale-up Investment: As small businesses become further established, there are opportunities for larger investment. Just like TV's Dragon's Den, investing in an enterprise means you can buy an equity share in the business the proceeds from which are used to help the business grow. This provides the opportunity for investors within the church or who are known to the church to become catalysts in scaling-up a business that has proved itself.

Small businesses make up the majority of all businesses in a country and are the foundation of even the biggest global economies. Remember small is beautiful and every big business was small at some point. Companies like Amazon began in a garage so just imagine what businesses your church could help start in a garage, garden shed kitchen table or church co-working space at this time.

Being the key driver in building businesses is transformational not only for the people running it, but for those who work within it

If you enjoyed this book, you can go deeper on
this transformation journey by signing up for our
Cinnamon Transformation Course,
available free at

cinnamonnetwork.com/course

Conclusion

My prayer is that this small book will make a big difference as your local church demonstrates Jesus's love in tangible ways to people experiencing vulnerability and that your community is transformed.

Each chapter offers new, strategic and practical ways for your church to be even more impactful in the community.

As we explored in the introduction, followers of Jesus are called to demonstrate the kingdom of God through the forgiveness of sin, social inclusion, economic empowerment and political justice.

Please let us know your stories of how God is working so we can tell others and inspire them so we can lean into this great adventure together.

Let us be God's hope givers!

About The Author

Matt Bird is a Global Speaker, Entrepreneur and Founder CEO of Cinnamon Network International helping churches transform communities.

He has spoken in 40 countries to more than a million people, authored more than a dozen books and is a regular broadcaster on radio, television and social media.

He is also the Founder CEO of Issachar Global helping people understand the times and how to live and lead, Relationology International helping leaders and their organisations build profitable relationships and Rebottling providing experiences of the greatest wines guided by the greatest sommeliers in the comfort of your home.

Matt lives in Wimbledon, England with his wife Esther and their three children.

Why not meet Matt online for a virtual coffee...

www.coffeewithmatt.com

About Cinnamon Network International

Cinnamon Network helps churches transform community.

- The **Cinnamon Transformation Pathway** supports churches to discern community needs and opportunities and replicate social enterprise projects with a track record for impact.

- The **Cinnamon Faith Action Audit** enables churches in a local government area to work together to measure their collective impact in order to catalyse their civic transformation journey.

- The **Cinnamon Spirit of Enterprise** resources churches to support people with ideas to start a businesses enterprise that creates social value, sustainable employment and economic growth.

Cinnamon Network International is developing resources and courses as well as networks in more than a dozen countries across four continents.

www.cinnamonnetwork.com

Other Books

Transformation

The Spirit of Enterprise

Replicate *(coming soon)*

www.mattbirdpublishing.com

Printed in Great Britain
by Amazon